ANCIENT GREECE

Troll Associates

ANCIENT GREECE

by Rae Bains

Illustrated by Hal Frenck

Troll Associates

Library of Congress Cataloging in Publication Data

Bains, Rae.
   Ancient Greece.

   Summary: Briefly traces the origins of modern western
culture in Greek civilization as it developed during
the thousand years before Christ.
   1. Greece—Juvenile literature.   [1. Greece.   2. Civilization, Greek.   3. Civilization, Ancient]   I. Frenck,
Hal, ill.   II. Title.
DF77.B24   1985   938   84-2685
ISBN 0-8167-0244-6 (lib. bdg.)
ISBN 0-8167-0245-4 (pbk.)

The culture of the modern western world can be traced back to the civilization of ancient Greece. There, more than 2,000 years ago, people studied science and mathematics. The ancient Greeks also produced great sculpture, architecture, pottery, and crafts. The poetry and drama of ancient Greece are still read and performed and studied today.

The great athletic contests called the Olympic games began in ancient Greece. And so did the most important contribution of all—the concept of democracy.

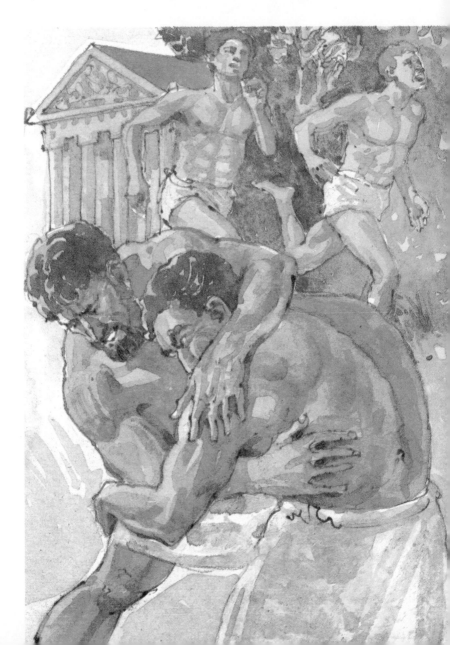

Ancient Greece was a rocky, hilly peninsula with a rough and rugged coastline marked by many natural harbors and inlets. The nearby islands, such as Crete, Corfu, Rhodes, and Samos, were also part of ancient Greece. Most of the population lived on the peninsula.

The ancient Greeks also had colonies across the Ionian Sea, in what is now Italy, and across the Aegean Sea, in what is present-day Turkey.

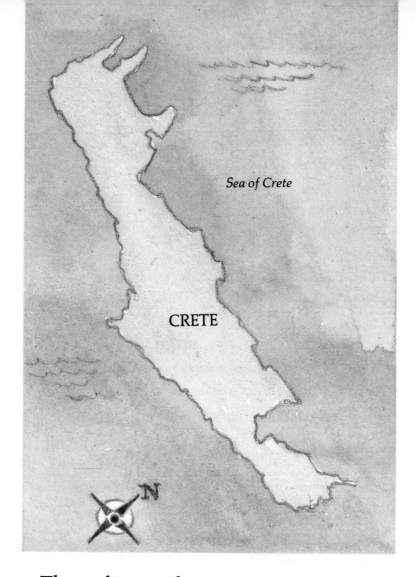

The earliest civilization in ancient Greece began on the island of Crete, in the Mediterranean. It was called the Minoan civilization, and it dates back approximately 5,000 years, to a period of time known as the Bronze Age.

Bronze is a metal composed of copper and tin. When the people on Crete learned to make weapons and armor of bronze, it gave them a significant advantage over other tribes. The other tribes were still using stone to make tools of war.

For about 2,000 years, the Minoan civilization flourished. During the reign of King Minos, the magnificent palace of Knossos was built. Knossos was the capital of Crete. The palace and the other elaborate buildings of Knossos were the basis of a famous Greek legend. It told about a huge labyrinth and the

Minotaur that lived in it. The labyrinth was a winding maze of underground passageways from which no one ever escaped. The Minotaur was a bull-like monster that killed any stranger who invaded its territory.

In time, the Minoan culture declined and Knossos was destroyed.

The Helladic civilization developed in Hellas, which was the mainland of Greece. It lasted for several hundred years. The stories of the remarkable Greek poet, Homer, tell of the last days of the Helladic period. These stories tell how the Helladic people of Greece fought against the Trojans, who lived in what is now the country of Turkey.

According to Homer, the war began when Paris, a Trojan prince, ran off with Helen, the wife of King Menelaus of Sparta. Agamemnon, king of Mycenae and brother of Menelaus, then led an army of Greeks against Troy. When the war ended many years later, Troy had been burned to the ground. But the war had weakened the Greeks, too.

Over the next few hundred years, many
different tribes swept down from the north
and destroyed the great civilization of
Mycenae. This period is sometimes called
the Dark Ages of Greek history. With the
passage of time, however, order and peace
returned to Greece.

By about 800 B.C., city-states began to develop. Each city-state consisted of a town surrounded by farms and grazing lands. At first, each town was just a fortress with a wall around it. When enemies approached, all the people took refuge inside the wall. Eventually, a second wall was built around the entire settlement.

City-states were of different sizes. The largest of all was Attica, also called Athens. It took more than a day for a traveler on foot to cross Athens. But some city-states were no more than tiny villages surrounded by a few miles of farm land. Nevertheless, large or small, each city-state was independent of the others.

Democracy was born in the Greek city-states, although ancient Greek democracy was not the same as modern democracy. All the adult male citizens of a city-state, such as Athens, shared in the government. Women were not permitted to vote. And slaves and foreigners were not regarded as citizens.

Citizens served as judges, council members, or government officials. Every job lasted one year. When two citizens had a legal quarrel, it might be heard by as many as 500 judges. These judges would vote on the decision, with the majority ruling. Nobody was paid for government service. It was considered the duty of every citizen to help to run the state.

One city-state, Sparta, was somewhat different from the others. Sparta was run along military lines, and Spartan citizens were full-time soldiers. They began training for military life when they were just seven years old. Reading and other forms of culture were not important parts of Spartan education, as they were in the other Greek city-states.

The farming, crafts, and industry of Sparta were in the hands of slaves, called Helots, and hired freemen. Crafts and industry were the work of the *perioeci*, who were freemen without votes. They lived in the villages, under the protection of the Spartans.

The long period of peace ended in the fifth century B.C.

Persia, under King Darius, ruled all of Asia Minor, including many Greek colonies. Not satisfied with this, King Darius declared war on Greece. A number of Greek city-states, led by Athens, fought against the Persian forces. Although greatly outnumbered, the Greeks defeated the Persians. The key to this victory was the superior Greek navy.

After the Persian Wars, Athens, with its powerful naval force, dominated the Greek city-states. It formed a league of city-states. Each league member paid for the protection of the Athenian military forces. This period of history is known as the Golden Age of Athens, noted for its peace and culture.

During the Golden Age, all the arts

flourished. The finest sculptors, such as Phidias and Myron, produced works of extraordinary classical beauty.

Architecture also flourished. The Parthenon and Erechtheum, two magnificent stone temples, were built on the Acropolis. The Acropolis is a hill in the center of Athens, where the fortress had originally stood.

The Golden Age was also noted for the philosophers Democritus and Socrates. Greek theater was at its height, staging the tragedies of Aeschylus, Sophocles, and Euripides, and the comedies of Aristophanes. Painting and music were equally well represented during the Golden Age, but almost none of it has survived the passage of time.

The peace and stability that fostered this magnificent culture also created prosperity for the Greeks. Though most of the farms were small and on poor soil, the farmers produced abundant crops of grapes, olives, grain, fruits, and vegetables. They also raised sheep, which supplied wool for much of their clothing.

In such cities as Athens, Corinth, and Miletus, fine craftsmen turned out pottery, jewelry, cloth, furniture, armor, and weapons, and many other manufactured goods. And the Greek merchant fleet engaged in extensive trade throughout the known world.

The Golden Age ended, however, when the other city-states rebelled against Athenian control. Sparta, the most warlike of the city-states, led the successful rebellion.

Though this long war, called the Peloponnesian War, resulted in victory for Sparta, it eventually caused the downfall of all the Greek city-states. Weakened by years of fighting, they came under the rule of a Macedonian tribesman, named Philip, from the north.

Philip of Macedonia and his son, Alexander the Great, ruled Greece until the middle of the fourth century B.C. In that time, Greek culture spread through much of

Europe, Asia, and Africa. But the ideals of democracy were erased during this period.

In the second century B.C., the Romans conquered Macedonia and Greece. Greece was now under Roman rule. But like all the conquerors before them, the Romans were strongly influenced by Greek art, culture, and religion.

The conquerors took many of the finest Greek sculptures back to Rome. They imitated Greek poetry, drama, and music. Even the Roman gods and goddesses were modeled on those of the Greeks.

In these and in so many other ways, the glory that was ancient Greece lived on through the centuries. And, in many ways, it is still with us today.